T0145040

Contrite Heart, Believer and Stroke

ANDREA ELIS WALKER

AuthorHouse™
1663 Liberty Drive
Bloomington, IN 47403
www.authorhouse.com
Phone: 1 (833) 262-8899

Because of the dynamic nature of the Internet, any web addresses or links contained in this book may have changed
since publication and may no longer be valid. The views expressed in this work are solely those of the author and do not
necessarily reflect the views of the publisher, and the publisher hereby disclaims any responsibility for them.

https://theprogenitor.com/history/shaka-zulu-biography-and-facts/
https://webuyblack.com/blog/queen-nandi-mother-shaka-zulu/
https://www.healthline.com/health/stroke-types#treatments
https://www.healthline.com/health/pancreatic-pseudocyst

This book is printed on acid-free paper.

Scripture quotations marked NIV are taken from the Holy Bible, New International Version®. NIV®.
Copyright © 1973, 1978, 1984 by International Bible Society. Used by permission of Zondervan. All rights reserved. [Biblica]

Scripture quotations marked KJV are from the Holy Bible, King James Version (Authorized Version).
First published in 1611. Quoted from the KJV Classic Reference Bible, Copyright © 1983 by The Zondervan Corporation.

Scripture quotations marked GNT are taken from the Good News Translation — Second Edition.
Copyright © 1992 by American Bible Society. Used by permission. All rights reserved.

Unless otherwise indicated, all scripture quotations are from The Holy Bible, English Standard Version® (ESV®).
Copyright ©2001 by Crossway Bibles, a division of Good News Publishers. Used by permission. All rights reserved.

Scripture taken from the New King James Version®. Copyright © 1982 by Thomas Nelson. Used by permission. All rights reserved.

ISBN: 978-1-6655-0613-7 (sc)
978-1-6655-0614-4 (e)

Print information available on the last page.

Published by AuthorHouse 11/04/2020

authorHOUSE®

Contrite Heart,

Believer *and* Stroke

My birth name is **Andrea Elis Walker,** and I am not a famous person, but I do love humanity. I was born and raised in Omaha, Nebraska 1969. There was no special event to mark my arrival. I am an average African American female given life from my mother Tanya Walker and father David Standifer. I have been given the duty to deliver this message about obstacles and tricks that could make you miss out on the blessings of God. It almost happened to me. But I ordained to have a God-centered life. My prayer is that readers use my experiences as insights and wisdom to renounce the plan of evil declarations over their life

My beginnings

I never liked my birth name but as I grew to love myself. I changed my perspective regarding that name. Ondie is my nickname. I chose it because many people mispronounced my given name. The simple name Andrea was Andie, Undie, Unnie, Undiewear, Pon-Pon, and many others. I grew tired of correcting people, so I chose and developed the name and spelling of Ondie. I wanted to be my authentic self.

As I grew older I was intrigued with African history and found my nickname in King Shaka Zulu's mother name — Nandi. This became a key component in my life.

Why?

Shaka Zulu was the leader of the Zulu kingdom from 1816 to 1828. Historically, he was one of the most influential monarchs in the Zulu kingdom. Queen Nandi the mother of Shaka Zulu Ndlorukazi Nandi kaBebe eLangeni (meaning The Sweet One) was born around 1760 in Langeni to a minor chief of the Langeni tribe, Bhebhe. She is widely considered to be one of the greatest single parents who ever lived. Nandi had to protect her son from famine, assassination attempts, and enemies. His step-father helped him train and become one of the greatest military minds of all time.

Early Childhood

I am the only child born to my mother Tanya Walker and father David Standifer. As teenagers my mother and father had a brief love affair. My father and his brother Rick attend a neighborhood party and that chance encounter set the stage for me to come into this world.

My father had been betrayed by his girlfriend who cheated on him with his best friend. His goal was to find someone to make him happy. Something clicked at that party and he decided to start a new relationship with the woman who became my mother. My mother didn't realize at the time that this was a rebound relationship. She later become privy to this fact when his former girlfriend (Valda) was found to be pregnant. It was my father's second child. The distrust and disloyalty made the love affair a short one. In spite of the fact that he never quite relinquished his heart from Valda, my father grew to love my mother. The circumstances weren't right for them, but eventually the relationship grew.

My mother became pregnant and my father stayed by her side because he loved her and his new baby girl. My mother almost died giving birth to me – that's why I'm her only child. The experience caused her to not have any more children. Although, I was my dad's second child, he did father others as well. I'm a sister to Teri, Cheri, Lafonda and a spiritually adopted daughter named Detra. I can say I had good relationship with all of my sisters, but it came with a price. My father was kept away from his daughters because of the relationship he had with my mother. My sisters' mother did not understand that God had purpose and plans for my father and the truth was that my sisters' mother was guilty of causing the wounds in my father's heart.

My father carried around pictures of his daughters which showed his love. Later, my grandmother, Sarah Cletus Standifer, allowed all of my sisters to come live with her. She tried to help raise them. Grandmother Cletus was similar to my mother in the since that she was very loving and wanted the best for all three of her boys and their children. My father was her baby boy.

Overall, I had good childhood experiences, lots of love from the people who were around me. Because of that love, it allowed me to be free to explore the world. My mother and father always saw the good in me. It was apparent because I was full of life. I knew I was supposed to be someone important. While growing up I was a dancer, actress, comedian, cook, athlete, bodybuilder, model, beauty pageant participant, tomboy.

My parents did not understand me and I really did not understand myself. God had given me so many gifts from birth. One of those gifts stood out from the many. That gift was the ability to see beyond human capability. I'd seen future events before they happened. I was clairvoyant, a.k.a. psychic.

Clairvoyant means, having or exhibiting an ability to perceive events in the future or beyond normal sensory contact.

I had a dream that two men wanted to break in our apartment. One of the men had on an orange jacket and the other a blue jacket. I was extremely frightened because I was at home by myself. My mother was working late. I picked up the phone to make a call to my grandmother's home for help, but I could not get through. There was no such thing as call-waiting and during those time the phone just gave a busy signal.

One of the two men threw a branch onto our patio which scared me. I tried calling my grandmother's home again and someone I didn't know answered and called my name. They said in a horrifying voice that they were going to kill me. I immediately woke up from this dream in terror.

I tried to alert my mother of the eminent danger, but she didn't listen to me. She thought of me as a child full of fantasy and too much TV watching. Two months later, two men as I described in the dream tried to break into our apartment. My mother was not home. I was terrified. I called my grandmother's home and was able to get through to my aunt Lisa Walker. I told her what was happening, and she drove over to my home to pick me up.

As I walked out the door and up the stairs there were those two men in the orange and blue jackets, and I told my aunt "There are the men trying to break into my home." My young heart was so scared and frightened by these events that when I arrived at my grandmother's home I immediately called my mother to tell her to watch out for the men who meant harm to us. Looking back in my life, I believe this gift was given to me as a measure of protection.

God never lets the enemy know what his plans are in this war for humanity. God knows beforehand what we will endure in this life, so he provides us with weapons. It's very important to distinguish between clairvoyance and the Holy Spirit. For the gifts and calling of God are without repentance. — Romans 11:29 KJV

Meaning gifts were freely given to all humanity. We are not required to do anything but be born, meaning that our children are gifts and they are valuable. Clairvoyance was given to me as a child. As I grew older I needed to understand my gifts because I never met anyone like me. God spoke to me clearly.

The Holy Spirit is God's power in action, his active force. (Micah 3:8; Luke 1:35) God sends out his spirit by projecting his energy to any place to accomplish his will. But you will receive power when the Holy Spirit comes on you (Acts 1:8 NIV) You might ask yourself the importance of this explanation to this book. It is to show you clearly the purpose and predestination of God. All this is a part of who the creator is and how he fights for humanity.

My upbringing was not God centered; I was not raised to know God. My father would share with me his experiences with God. He was Seventh-day Adventist. My grandmother, Venita Walker, was a Jehovah's Witness and required me to spend time studying the Bible with a group of family witnesses. None of them knew that I had been communicating with God all of my life. God had been counselling and protecting me and I grew to love him.

As a child I never told anyone about this gift to see future events for fear of being ridiculed or being categorized as crazy. This gift as child was quite strange and sometimes frightening due to the dreams and visions I experienced. .As a child I slept with my mother for fear that something was trying kill me in my sleep. My fear of darkness arose from what I seen through the visions and dreams.

I was highly sought after by the Kingdom of Satan. Combine the gift along with being tormented at night by witches and evil spirits, darkness for me was not enjoyable. (I must mention that my mother was infatuated with horror films and Hollywood and would subject me to watch them).

When God showed me things to come by dreams, I normally would pay very close attention to what the dream was trying to show me and yet at the same time be secretive about what it was revealing to me. I hid these revelations from everyone — even my parents. I became used to dreams and visions happening in my life. I was becoming aware of what is called the supernatural.

If you are one of those type of people who do not believe in good or evil, heaven or hell, then your spiritual eyes have not been opened. There is an unseen world that we live in and there is a war that is happening daily

For our struggle is not against flesh and blood, but against the rulers, against the authorities, against the powers of this dark world and against the spiritual forces of evil in the heavenly realms. — Ephesian 6:12 NIV

Being a parent is a great responsibility. It is similar to being like God. You are the example for children to look to. We as God's children are the salt of this earth. We must protect our children. Raise them to know God. Fight for them in prayer. Stand against perversion. Children are a gift from God; they are his reward. Children born to a young man are like sharp arrows to defend him.Psalms 127

There is an evil in this world and it wants to kill, steal and destroy all of humanity. This evil wants to corrupt the purpose of God through humanity.

SEASON ONE

As a young girl

The summer I almost died is an experience I will never forget.

It was a beautifully sunny, hot day and I went along with my Aunt Lisa to Gallagher Park (a local swimming pool). I was about 8 years old. I was excited to plunge into that cool refreshing water. Like most children, I loved getting in the water. A lot of our neighborhood friends were there and that made me more excited to go have fun and play. The smaller children were restricted to certain areas of the pool because of our height.

Our swimming ability was probably a factor as well. While I was restricted to the side of the pool that was five feet and shallower, my Aunt Lisa, who was taller and could swim, was among the older, experienced bathers.

I jumped in the pool and splashed around without fear. Even though I didn't know how to swim, I knew how to float and hold my breath. Lisa left me to play with my friends and went right in the pool and started to swim. As the pool became more crowded, she wanted to keep an eye on me. She brought me over to her side of the pool on her shoulders.

I began to get a little fearful because this was a new experience. I trusted her, but she was taking me to a side that had deeper water and a place in the pool that I had never been. There were a lot of older children on that side of the pool so Lisa focused on holding onto me. Suddenly another teen came swimming by her she lost her footing and slipped in the water. I fell into the water.

I panicked and started to grab at anything I could hold onto. But there was nothing there — not even Lisa. As I began to sink to the bottom of the pool, I could see nothing but water. There was nothing solid, nothing stable. Water everywhere. I inhaled water into my lungs and felt the burning sensation of a substance that wasn't supposed to be there. I surrendered to my fate, but Stephanie Harrison (neighborhood friend) grabbed me out of the pool and laid me on the concrete. Immediately began CPR – breathing life back into my body. In those moments of despair, I felt myself disappearing from existence. I did not know what to do. I can't say that I prayed or called on God. I just let the water engulf me and let my life slip away. I did contemplate what was next for me – where my spirit and Life would end up.

Until that point had set in motion the destination for my immortal soul. I did, however, fear for my Aunt Lisa. She'd be in trouble from my mother and grandmother for not protecting me. I never spoke about the incident to anyone, least of all the two women who I believed loved me the most. I didn't want to bring harm to my aunt even though she had unintendedly brought harm to me. The two of us were more like sisters. I did not want her harmed. Besides up until that incident, we were having a good day.

That near-death experience opened my eyes to the possibility of death at any moment and that resonated in my soul. I would go on to other experiences that put me near death's door. That was my first glimpse of mortality made me recognize that something greater than anything I could comprehend wanted me alive. I felt a sense of protection that didn't come from a human being.

I was baptized in the name of Jesus at the age of 13 because I was compelled to know God better so I could understand my gift and all of the questions I had about my life. Emotionally I felt my life would be better after baptism. Physically I had been freed from the torment of reasoning and fret about my life. However, that feeling soon came to an end because of peer pressure. I developed beauty over time My attractiveness brought to me young and older men. I was never able to see my attractiveness because I was never told that I was pretty or attractive except by my mother. My father never told me for fear of what I would grow to be. My theory on why he did not acknowledge was to serve as a protective measure.

Another reason I wanted to get to know God better was that I did not like the real-life situations that I was assigned. It would seem as if God dealt me a deck of cards that were useless. I felt I needed to live a more fulfilled life before my commitment to God. I was now 15 and all of my peers were partying and having sex. I experienced those things too and I was not thrilled by any of it. I was a home body and babysitter. I yearned for more of what life could offer me.

Time and experiences were given to me to commit my life to Gods kingdom. I was living an uncommitted life at that time. I had opened myself to the Kingdom of Satan by being baptized in the name of Jesus. I did not realize that this uncommitted lifestyle would drive me to attempt to take my life at the age of 15. And Peter said to them, "Repent and be baptized every one of you in the name of Jesus Christ for the forgiveness of your sins, and you will receive the gift of the Holy Spirit. — Acts 2:38 ESV

Suicide and Why

At the age of 15 my mother moved us from Myott Park to Meredith Park. They were both low income apartment complexes. At that time, Omaha was like many other metropolitan areas trying to do away with housing projects. The National Housing Act sought encourage the development of a diverse community. By interspersing low-income renters among middle class homeowners, there would be a broad range of interests and backgrounds. The hope was that the community would be totally integrated, socially and economically.

Myott Park was completed in 1975 as an attempt at scattered site housing. It quickly became just as rundown as the projects. Huge patches of dirt emerged where grass once grew. The seemingly toney wooden structures didn't hold up well to the Nebraska weather – sub zero temperatures in winter and 100-degree days in summer. They were configured in confusing ways and guests often got lost trying to locate apartments of friends and relatives. I'm not sure the experiment of foisting the have-nots onto the haves really worked. Myott Park began to get a reputation for being a hard place to live and that was the driving force behind our relocation. That move was like all hell breaking loose in our lives.

It is so unbelievable that you can be birth from your parent and that they could not sense the pain and torment you go through losing your friends. I was unhappy with the move but happy that life seemed to be turning for the better. My sadness came by losing my sense of surroundings. My mother did not realize the place she chose to move us in was nice and accommodating, the environment was full of ungodliness. The developers took the old Monmouth Park Elementary and turned them into cute apartment.(Meredith Park Apartments) They even left the chalkboards. The new-home smell masked the evil lurking in just about every corridor. Satan was using that environment and demonic host to drive me to take my life because I felt so emotionally alone.

My mother moved us into a place of the unknown thinking that I would feel safer close to my grandmother Sarah Cletus home. My mother believed in God but believed in reality more. She was not of faith like my dad and grandmother were. The people that dwelled in Monmouth Park Apartments were doing some things that were considered immoral. Because of who God called me to be, my spirit was sensitive to that which was not of God. Satan was using that building to haunt me and drive me to take my life. God showed me his power through rescuing me and I did not have to take my life.It was then I began to take a real focused look on who God was. I truly desired to have a committed life and live for God but this season in my life CONVINCED me that God and the Devil are real.

How God rescued me

I was unable to sleep one night and as usual I frequently worried about my future. I sensed an unusual presence there in the home with me. I prayed but this presence would not go away and I could not stop this evil presence from speaking to me. It made me feel filthy and unprotected. I even prayed that it would go away but it persisted and began to show me images of me dying and how I could take my life and because

I had no power over this evil I bowed to the belief that death was my only option. I went to the kitchen and I got some hard liquor as I thought that maybe I could drown this voice out of my head. All of these measurements taken did not do anything so anxiety took over me and I went into the bathroom to see if my mother had any sedatives, but she did not any. I was crying heavily and talking to God at the same time. I picked up the phone to call for some help but who could I call? no one believed that evil presence existed except one man who was married to my cousin Deborah Wilson. His name was Pastor Allious Gee, but I was not able to reach him by phone. No one was answering the phone. I did not realize that I was being tormented by this evil presence.

At that moment I made up my mind that I would kill myself by slitting my wrist, but I could not do that without explaining to my mother that I loved her and appreciated her. I went into her bedroom and found her best friend Lynette Lewis sleeping in her room. I turned around and went back into the living room and sat on the couch and called Al Gee again. At that same moment Lynette was up sleep walking. She walked toward me as if she was in the army and she turned and stepped onto our dining room chair and then on to the table. She lifted her hands and began to verbalize something that I could not hear but I knew she was praying. That went on for a few minutes and she then stepped down off the table and chair and went back in the room. I was completely blown away by this, God already knew to have help for me that day. I did not realize that I was not fighting alone. I went back to the phone and called Al Gee again — this time he answered. I told him about my suicide attempt and said I needed to talk to him in person. Before I hung up my mother came home and saw my distress. She was concerned and confused, but I knew there was nothing she could do. I hugged her tightly and told her I loved her. Then I dashed out the door, heading to the church to see Al Gee.

I didn't stop to look in the mirror to check my hair and makeup. I didn't look at my clothes to make sure they were presentable. I didn't care what I looked like. My previous mindset of looking pretty and having a whole bunch of boys chasing after me was left behind. I was on my way to being committed to God. I now knew that Pastor Gee could help me get what I needed from God, The Holy Spirit. I walked a few miles from 30th Ames Avenue to 2901 Miami Street. Although I took a pretty straight route, it took more than 2 hours to get there. Pastor Al Gee was waiting on me.

When I arrived at the Faith Deliverance church. Al Gee was waiting and greeted me with his calming smile. I immediately started to sob and cry as I felt ashamed that I had taken steps to end my life .He looked at me and said with a firm voice "Ondie, you know that the devil is a liar, Right" I said crying "Yes" He said you need to be filled with the Holy Spirit. I replied "Yes". Those words freed me. He gave me instructions to come back to church as often as I could to tarry for the Holy Spirit. Those words and my actions started me on a journey of survival and living for the Most High God. I knew I was on my way to that better life that I had been yearning for.

In this same season Satan became so angry with me because he could not take my life, dreams and hope. He changed his focus onto my mother.

Motherless child

The road wasn't without detours. As my mother moved closer to God, the lure of the devil became stronger. She didn't see the harm in going out to a bar with her younger sister, Theresa Walker. But that was her last day on earth. She was killed in October 1986.

It was as if the life I had begun to develop was suddenly destroyed. I became numb and emotionless. I had never envisioned a life without my mother. I had always planned that she would grow old and have me to take care of her. I wanted to buy her a house one day. I wanted wanted to place my children in her arms for her to love on them.

I gained an understanding of how Satan tries to cut off the plan & purpose of God through death.

SEASON TWO

My Marriage

Whoso find a wife find a good thing and obtain favor of the Lord. — Prov 18

I want to tell you always look to God to answer your questions when it comes to marriage. I was 19 years of age when I met my husband. I always knew that God was going to bless me, but I did not want to marry just anyone. I was enjoying my life as a single young woman. I had found some answers in life through the word of God. I had begun to heal from the great pain and sorrow of my mother's death. Life was moving in the right direction. I'd planned to go see a movie by myself at the Westroads Mall. As a single woman secure in who she was and what she wanted, I had no problem doing things on my own. I didn't feel that I needed a man to justify me. My perspective on life had gotten that good.

I ran into a dear friend named Michelle who was meeting her husband Kevin Goodwin and his brother Bryon Goodwin to see a movie. It had been a while since we'd been around each other and she was overjoyed to see me. The feeling was mutual. I was ready to embrace friends again. She invited me to join them and said her brother-in-law wasn't with a date. It would be part a nice little double date.

The brother-in-law was an attractive man, but I was not stirred with any great desire to go on this impromptu date. I had been dating other men within my church and was sure they were the type in my future. I still had dreams of a stable home with a husband and children. I really didn't even want to see the movie that had picked out. It was a horror flick called "Child's Play." I'm not a fan of scary movies as it is, and I certainly didn't think Satanic messages and images would be entertaining. I agreed to go despite my reservations. It was more a desire to spend time with Michelle than to get to know Bryon.

Playing matchmaker, Michelle sat me next to her brother-in-law. I had very few words for him. I was vexed in my spirit with watching this evil movie. To make matters worse, Kevin and Bryon got into an altercation with some younger men in the movie theater. The entire experience was a big turn off. Once the movie ended, we walked to our cars. Michelle took me aside and asked if I thought Bryon was cute.

"He's O.K.," I replied. She did not realize that I had dated an NBA player and had turned down a marriage proposal him and several other men. Sure, I was in the market for a husband, but having had been with Saks of Fifth Avenue, why would I settle for Target? But then I saw how happy she was with her mate and realized that she really wanted me to have that same kind of happiness. A man's bank account isn't the only measure of his worth, I thought. There was a reason why I had turned down those other guys. Perhaps God was telling me to give this brother a chance. I said goodbye to the trio and invited Bryon to come by job. I worked at the men's fragrance counter at Dillard's department store and wanted him to come check out some new scents. It turns out that Michelle told Bryon that I was well off financially. I'm not sure if he'd have been that into me otherwise. But he did come by Dillard's to shop a Father's Day gift.

Without going into a lot of details about the debacle that was our marriage, I'll just say that I didn't trust my own instincts. After we were married, I tried to make it work because I never wanted to be in this life alone without a husband. I was a prepared young woman for marriage but he was not a prepared man. I will let it be known that I never wanted to be divorced and forced into a system of sex without being married. That is what God calls fornication.

Eventually I put more of my trust in God to help me overcome. I let go of unforgiveness or offenses as soon as they come. I realized that I allowed the trick of the enemy to deceive me into marrying a man that was not ready to leave and cleave to his wife. I love many of his family members and some are the reason I'm living today. From their prayers and the body of Christ.

Years Later after our divorce I explained to my my ex-husband that I forgave him awhile ago my life and times are in Gods hand. — Psalm 31:15 I had to acknowledge to myself that I had also been deceived during my marriage because he believed the lies that were spoken about me. This played a significant role in dismantling our marriage. I was not prepared emotionally to deal with this chaotic marriage. I was done being the person that was wanting peace in that relationship and peace between the two church organizations who separated us. This season I learned to deal with the lies that were told about me. I also learned to walk away from a fictional love based on mentality of the carnal mind.

These chapters give the reader a glimpse into my life and what makes me a unique woman of God — my true self. I have gained a wealth of knowledge through my life experiences. I have no worries nor regrets. All of those challenges were required to birth out the woman that I am today. I have fought and still fighting many family generational curses. I am aware that salvation and holiness is for the will of the person to accept or reject. I cannot designate heaven or hell to any person because I am not God. The only reason why I am living to write this book is because of the Mercy and Grace of God. I do not count myself to be any more than what God spoke me to be.

> Even if a whole army surrounds me, I will not be afraid; even if enemies attack me, I will still trust God. — Psalms 27:3 GNT

> Have you considered Job, there is none like him on earth a perfect and upright man. He fears God and he turns away from evil. — Job 1:6

The cause and effect are my reasoning to stay away from sin (evil). It has always been the consequences as warning signs for me .If you are graced with longevity you will see that the plan of God supersedes man's plans and his wisdom God balances out your life when you yield to him. The book of Job explains life and encounters for the child of God. God brags about his children and gives them favor. The revelation in this book is that God adores humanity that follow his commandments and Satan hates them. Satan sets out to test how much you love God. God allows this because he knows what you are made of. You were made for the challenge and you have weapons through the Holy Spirit. The test is to show which side you will choose, good or evil. The father God, walks with you every step of the way. Another great book worthy of studying is the Book of Ruth Naomi's feeling of destitution depicts how I felt about my life, "Turn again daughters go your way for I am too old to have a husband." — Ruth 1:1-22

I once was young and married and I experienced great loss due to suffering a miscarriage and marital disappointment. I did not realize that these incidents were setting the tone of my life of pain and sorrow. In Naomi's statement to her daughter in laws explained how I felt about life, people and God

"Go your way" this was my attitude towards life,I felt abandoned by God.

How I felt emotionally played a big role as to how I felt about God and life as a man thinketh in his heart, so is he." Proverb 23:7 KJV

God moves beyond your doubt and disparity, when you have encountered unfairness of life, mistakes and chaos for I know the plans I have for you," declares the LORD, "plans to prosper you and not to harm you, plans to give you hope and a future. Jeremiah 29:11 NIV

Words cannot express his love for humanity

"For God so loved the world, that he gave his only begotten Son, that whosoever believeth in him should not perish, but have everlasting life."John 3:16 KJV

His Reconciliation is unfathomable.

that is, that God was in Christ reconciling the world to Himself, not [a]imputing their trespasses to them, and has committed to us the word of reconciliation. Corinthians 5:19 NKJV

Dec 21,2017 was the day that my life would change drastically. In 2000 I was diagnosed with a pancreas pseudo cyst which I had inherited through my genetics. A pancreatic pseudocyst is a type of cyst is contained inside an enclosed sac of its own with an epithelium lining. Instead, the pseudocyst forms within a cavity or space inside the pancreas and is surrounded by fibrous tissue. Pancreatic pseudocysts do contain inflammatory pancreatic fluid (particularly the digestive enzyme amylase) or semisolid matter. There are several different types of pancreatic cysts. Some pancreatic cysts result from certain rare diseases, such as von Hippel-Lindau disease (a genetic disorder). This was what my pseudo cyst was.

I suffered with this medical condition since I was a child and it caused my digestive issues on into my adulthood. During 1990's int 2014 there were very limited medical options in Omaha Nebraska with this diagnosis. The options were surgery to remove half of pancreas and spleen, Aspiration or live with the pain. I made the decision to keep my weight down and by faith keep my spleen and pancreas intact based on the word of God. By his stripes we are healed Isaiah 53:5.

In October 2014 I sold my home in Omaha,Nebraska and moved to Florida because I planned to die in a beautiful place. My belief that I was going to die was because of my diagnosis. My choice to live by faith was one I suffered through. I was in agony, daily living off of digestive enzymes, and Dr Christopher's pancreas formula and baby food. My weight fluctuated from160 to 210 pounds. I ate baby food because that is all my body could tolerate

My initial move to Florida was based on the belief that I finally could make some of my dreams come true before I died. While in Florida I endured obstacles, which impacted my life. One of those obstacles was the loss of my job due to illness. Losing employment did disrupt my life because I was in a new city and no one to help me.

My mindset was I felt that I could handle the stress as I had been through this type of loss before, so I did not allow fear to drive me into a panic mode. Second obstacle was prior to moving to Florida I fell in love with someone. I will discuss this type of love in an upcoming book titled <u>love and the purpose of God (published 2021)</u> The man was a believer but was not a Holy Spirit believer. The pain of not being with him caused significant emotional and mental stress on top of the job loss. I prayed that God would allow me to marry him. However, through the Holy Spirit, the answer was "No" to my request. I could not understand the reasoning behind Gods answer. My lack of understanding did not allow me to emotionally let go because I loved this man and I planned for him to be in my life since I was 12 years old. I justified the feelings I felt by praying harder and longer hoping that God would change his answer but God never changed his answer. I had to learn to rest assure in God word

> For my thoughts are not your thoughts, neither are your ways my ways, declares the LORD
> — ISAIAH 55:8 NIV

Being emotionally entangled in this human experience of Love, I could not unravel myself out of. I could not mentally or emotionally deal with loving someone that I could not have. On Dec 21, 2017, I went driving at night trying to gain an understanding as to "Why I could not get him out of my head and spirit.' There was no real rational reason that I should not be able to win him over to Christ. It did not make sense that God said no to my request for having him as a husband. This reasoning made me an emotional reck and I did not know what to do.

I experienced Sorrow that I could not express to anyone except God. This sorrow I felt I had not experienced since my mother's death and the loss of my child. I was broken beyond repair. No one would ever know how hurt I was because I mastered masking my pain through staying busy and making people think that love would never conquer me again. The truth was that being in love was what I always wanted.

Dec. 21, 2017 I had an emotional breakdown while driving. I had slipped out of reality. I watched the car go in slow motion and avoid a semi-truck that was merging into traffic. I became frightened but I kept driving onto the nearest medical facility Tampa General hospital. I cannot tell you what made me drive to the hospital but I did. I parked my vehicle and walked into emergency facility to gain help. I was given a nurse to assist me as I was bleeding profusely from my nose and mouth.

I woke up several months later from an induced coma. I was alone in a private room. I was fearful as to what happened to me I then became consciously aware of myself and I was alive and that I had no movement of my body and I was paralyzed. I cried, and in my mind I felt crushed as if I had been in a major car accident. I had no voice so I prayed and asked, " God Why did this happen to me?" I was a strong believer, Holy Spirit filled and trusted God to do the miraculous.

In my mind I started to list off things to God that I had done for the kingdom Christ:

- Prayed for the sick,
- Ushered people i to the kingdom of Christ
- Cared for children
- Gave money and time to the homeless,
- Opened my home to the homeless,
- Cooked and gave food to people in need.
- I did what I could humanly do for churches and humanity.
- Disciplined myself

After I finished that complaint to God, the Holy Spirit answered and said 'You Shall not die but live and declare the works of the lord. Psalms 118:17

I began to get quiet and settled in my head and spirit to listen to what the spirit was speaking to my soul. This yielding to the spirit of God brought me peace. I could do nothing but obey the word of God and repent as I had not walked in all of the calling that God gave me to do which was to preach and teach his word. The truth was I was living way below and surviving outside of what God told me to do for the body of Christ which is his Kingdom. I was disobedient to his calling, but God granted me mercy because he loved me. He had set the reset button in my life. The Holy Spirit then began to explain why I had suffered so much trauma in my life from the time I was born. The spirit began to show me why I faced many traumatic events in my life Electrocution, gun shots, fighting, car accidents, several rape attempts, hatred, jealousy, envy, malice, marital and child abuse, several near airplane crashes. Satan desired to sift me as wheat but God kept me by mercy and grace. It was my unique design that Satan could not penetrate. The chemical balance in my body and brain. My body was wired to sustain the pressures of life. I take no glory as a human being. The glory belongs to Jesus.

"I praise you because I am fearfully and wonderfully made; your works are wonderful, I know that full well." — Psalm 139:14 NIV

In 1990 I was diagnosed with a pancreatic pseudo cyst. This stroke was intensified due to my previous non-surgical repair of my pancreas pseudo cyst. Working in the medical industry for 14 years I recognized that by me being a left and right brain person, it was significantly harder for the stroke to cause death. The ischemic stroke is an illness and does not have the ability to think on its own it is a deliberate attack on the body to either to cause death or disability. The stroke that I endured caused my disability.

A stroke is a medical emergency that happens when the blood flow to your brain is interrupted. Without blood, your brain cells start to die. When I was able to read my medical report I realized how blessed I was to be alive. I am not just anybody I am the selected of God.

The feelings of pain and despair started to dissipate. I felt so much love and joy inside as the Holy Spirit continued to minister to my spirit. These are some of the spiritual factors leading causes in stroke behavior: heartbreak and disappointment, depression. What I experienced was as much spiritual as physical.

I accepted Jesus Christ as my savior but I rejected him regarding my emotional well-being. All of my life since I was a little girl. I wanted to be married, have children, a puppy and a home. Once I had those things, I still felt unfulfilled. I left my husband in 1993 and divorced him in 1995. I lost my biological child with him, and I moved on as if this was not killing me. Emotionally I shut down because I could do no more. I still believed God for a miracle of restoration and I took my wounded soul and buried myself in work and church.

I never understood the magnitude of love God had for me until I experienced the stroke. I used to equate how people treated me to how God felt towards me, but I had been absolutely mistaken. The people who said unkind words to me gave me no reasoning or perspectives as to why they said those words. Subconsciously the reason to deliver toxicity is from Jealousy,envy and hatred to get you to recant your testimony. This is what evil toxic people do,they do the work of their father the Devil. For many years I pretended that I was not wounded by their treatment and words. Yet I was being wounded day by day. I am so glad God sees everything. He is my vindicator.

The Reset Button

The mercy and favor of God is not fair.

> I will have mercy on whom I will have mercy, and I will have compassion on whom I will have compassion — Romans 9:15 KJV

I am alive today because of this mercy and compassion which is his favor. I had spent the majority of my life believing that all the bad things happened to me because I had done something wrong in life, but the truth is that I had done things right according to God and he was pleased. All of my labor was not in vain. God accepted my repentance and is allowing me to live because of it.

This grace and mercy is so much more than anyone can describe in words. It is favor. I am thankful and grateful of everything God has given me. The most wonderful outcome from all of this was God had plans and purpose for me. God set purpose in me by allowing me to be an only child so that he could pour into me the drive to survive and endurance.

> So, I say, walk by the Spirit, and you will not gratify the desires of the flesh. For the flesh desires what is contrary to the Spirit, and the Spirit what is contrary to the flesh. They are in conflict with each other, so that you are not to do whatever you want. — Galatians 5:16-17 NIV

> Trust in the Lord with all thine heart and lean not unto thine own understanding. — Prov 3 KJV

Conclusion

In conclusion the experiences has showed you segments of my life and as life continues further for me, I'm looking forward to my future. I'm working smarter not harder to maintain wise decisions. Parents pay attention to your children allow them to speak their mind. The message throughout this book is to help you find your way to living a successful life through the leading of the Holy Spirit. The word of God is life to those who believe. Allow these words that I explained of my life inspire you to live your best life in Christ Jesus. Then said they unto him, What shall we do, that we might work the works of God? Jesus answered them, This is the work of God, that you believe on him whom he hath sent. — John 6:28 KJV

I had struggled in life trying to fulfill the works of God when works could not save me. Allow God to complete the process of salvation in you.

Howbeit when he, the Spirit of truth, is come, he will guide you into all truth: for he shall not speak of himself; but whatsoever he shall hear, that shall he speak: and he will shew you things to come. — John 16-15 KJV

Then Jesus said, "Father, forgive them, for they do not know what they do." And they divided His garments and cast lots.

Thankfulness, Gratefulness and Forgiveness

I am so thankful to God that he does not remember my sins and does not hold me hostage to them as far as the east is from the west, so far has he removed our transgressions from us. —Psalms 103 NIV

I am grateful that I am covered by the baptism in Jesus name. — Acts 2:38

These two undisputable truths is why I forgive those that trespass against me. I yield to every word of God, if God forgave me, then who am I not to forgive others. I understand God and why he says "no" to some things we pray about.

Workbook

Retrace your childhood

How did your parents treat you

How did you learn about Money,sex,Law

What do you do for hobbies

How are you unique to this world

Are you prepared for Life

How is your hygiene

How is your eating habits

How healthy are you

What do you like to do for fun

How important is God to you

Printed in the United States
By Bookmasters